and a kang

National Gallery of Australia

kangaroo

wambuyn

rock python

nawaran

possum

marrngu

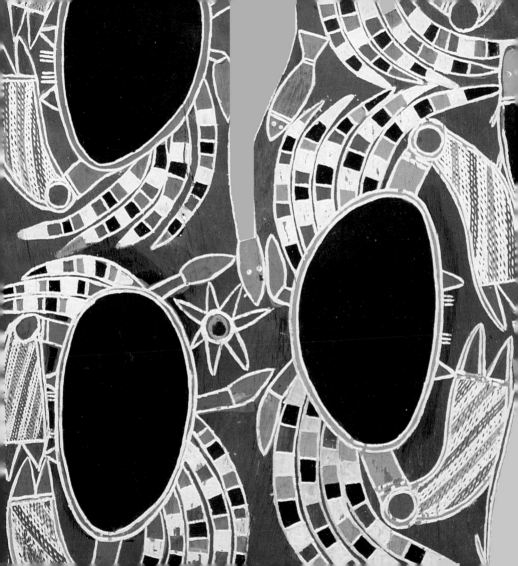

crab

nyoka'

butterfly

bon_ba

flying fox

warrnyu

eel-tailed catfish

bikurr

emu

gugaamgan

sea eagle

ngak ngak

saltwater crocodile

baru

spider

garr

blue-tongue lizard

dhamaling

fly

wurrurlurl

fish

guya

echidna

ninaar

python

pilkati

sawfish

yugwurrendangwa

ibis

garrala

magpie geese

gurrumatji

goanna

carda

crow

wäk

barramundi

namarnkol

shark

balangu

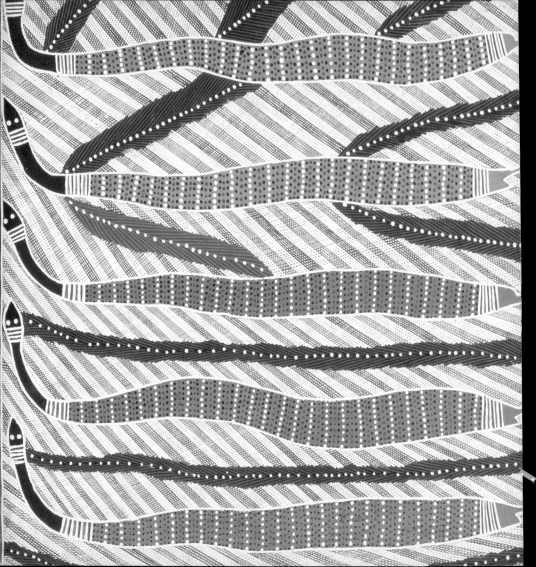

black-headed python

gunungu

long-necked
tortoise

minhala

saltwater fish

gapila

There are many different Aboriginal languages and the translations provided in this book are those from the language group of each artist where their work appears. Included in the following list are artists' language groups and the place in which each work was made. Measurements are given height before width. All works illustrated are from the Aboriginal and Torres Strait Islander Collection of the National Gallery of Australia.

kangaroo (wambuyn)
Milton Budge
Dhangadi people
Australia born 1941
Hunter and roo 1989 (detail)
Kempsey, New South Wales
synthetic polymer paint on canvas
54.0 x 119.0 cm

rock python (nawaran
Jimmy Midjaw Midjaw
Kunwinjku people
Australia 1897–1985
*Rock Python c.*1963 (detail)
Minjilang (Croker Island), West Arnhem Land, Northern Territory
natural pigments on eucalyptus bark
77.5 x 67.0 cm
Founding Donors Fund 1984

possum (marnngu)
Narritjin Maymuru
Manggalili people
Australia *c.*1922–1981
Jörg Schmeisser
Stolp, Germany born 1942
Possum 1978 (detail)
Canberra, Australian Capital Territory
intaglio
20.0 x 25.0 cm
Gift of Jörg Schmeisser 1986

crab (nyoka')
Tom Djawa
Gupapuyngu people
Australia 1905–1980
Crabs 1969 (detail)
Milingimbi, Central Arnhem Land, Northern Territory
natural pigments on eucalyptus bark
101.0 x 47.8 cm

butterfly (bonba)
Jack Wunuwun
Djinang people
Australia 1930–1990
Banambirr, The Morning Star 1987 (detail)
Gamerdi, Central Arnhem Land, Northern Territory
natural pigments on eucalyptus bark
178.0 x 125.0 cm
Purchased from National Gallery admission charges
© The estate of Jack Wunuwun
LPR Maningrida Arts and Culture

flying fox (warrnyu)
George Milpurrurru
Ganalbingu people
Australia born 1934
Flying foxes 1982 (detail)
Ramingining, Central Arnhem Land,
Northern Territory
natural pigments on eucalyptus bark
148.5 x 85.0 cm

eel-tailed catfish (bikurr)
Jack Kala Kala
Rembarrnga people
Australia 1932–1987
Sacred dilly bags 1983 (detail)
Maningrida, Central Arnhem Land,
Northern Territory
natural pigments on eucalyptus bark
111.0 x 68.0 cm

emu (gugaamgan)
Robert Campbell Jnr
Dhangadi/Ngaku people
Australia 1944–1993
Mary Durouse Australia
R Button Australia
Karen Smith Australia
David Fernando Australia
M Bridge Australia
Tribal totems 1989 (detail)
Kempsey, New South Wales
stencil
59.9 x 47.6 cm
Gordon Darling Fund 1989
Reproduced courtesy Roslyn Oxley9 Gallery

sea eagle (ngak ngak)
Ginger Riley Munduwalawala
Mara people
Australia born *c.*1937
Ngak Ngak, sea eagle 1988 (detail)
Ngukurr, South East Arnhem Land,
Northern Territory
synthetic polymer paint on canvas
90.0 x 121.0 cm
Moët and Chandon Fund 1991

saltwater crocodile (baru)
George Milpurrurru
Ganalbingu people
Australia born 1934
Bare the Crocodile 1993 (detail)
Ramingining, Central Arnhem Land,
Northern Territory
natural pigments on eucalyptus bark
147.0 x 72.0 cm

spider (garr)
George Milpurrurru
Ganalbingu people
Australia born 1934
Spider Dreaming 1985 (detail)
Ramingining, Central Arnhem Land,
Northern Territory
natural pigments on eucalyptus bark
144.0 x 114.5 cm

blue-tongue lizard (dhamaling)
Paddy Dhathangu
Liyagalawumirr people
Australia 1915–1993
Dhamaling (Blue-tongued lizards) 1983 (detail)
Ramingining, Central Arnhem Land,
Northern Territory
natural pigments on eucalyptus bark
67.0 x 34.5 cm

fly (wurrurlurl)
Don Gundinga
Djinang people
Australia 1941–1989
The artist's totems c.1979 (detail)
Ramingining, Central Arnhem Land,
Northern Territory
natural pigments on eucalyptus bark
122.0 x 61.5 cm

fish (guya)
George Garrawun
Djinang people
Australia 1945–1993
Freshwater fish c.1979 (detail)
Maningrida, Central Arnhem Land,
Northern Territory
natural pigments on eucalyptus bark
158.3 x 74.0 cm

echidna (ninaar)
Pooaraar
Charnuk people
Australia born 1939
Turtles 1988 (detail)
Canberra, Australian Capital Territory
relief
50.2 x 43.8 cm
Purchased from National Gallery
admission charges

python (pilkati)
Jack Kunti Kunti
Pintupi people
Australia c.1930–1990
Two snakes 1984 (detail)
Kintore, Western Desert, Northern Territory
synthetic polymer paint on canvas
100.5 x 184.0 cm
Founding Donors' Fund

sawfish (yugwurrendangwa)
Nandabitta
Anindilyakwa people
Australia 1911–1981
The Angurugu River 1970 (detail)
Groote Eylandt, Northern Territory
natural pigments on eucalyptus bark
64.9 x 35.6 cm

ibis (garrala)
Jack Wunuwun
Australia 1930–1990
Djinang people
Morning Star 1989 (detail)
Gamerdi, Central Arnhem Land,
Northern Territory
natural pigments on canvas
184.0 x 161.0 cm
© The estate of Jack Wunuwun
LPR Maningrida Arts and Culture

magpie geese (gurrumatji)
George Milpurrurru
Ganalbingu people
Australia born 1934
Gumang Magpie Geese 1987 (detail)
Ramingining, Central Arnhem Land,
Northern Territory
natural pigments on eucalyptus bark
163.0 x 74.0 cm

goanna (carda)
Pooaraar
Charnuk people
Australia born 1939
Final showdown 1987 (detail)
Cairns, Queensland
relief
46.1 x 32.5 cm

crow (wäk)
Paddy Dhathangu
Liyagalawumirr people
Australia 1915–1993
Wäk (Crows) 1983 (detail)
Ramingining, Central Arnhem Land,
Northern Territory
natural pigments on eucalyptus bark
78.0 x 54.0 cm

barramundi (namarnkol)
Jimmy Midjaw-Midjaw
Kunwinjku people
Australia 1897 –c.1985
Two barramundi c.1963 (detail)
Minjilang (Croker Island), West Arnhem Land,
Northern Territory
natural pigments on eucalyptus bark
56.0 x 76.0 cm

shark (balangu)
Dorothy Galaledba
Gunartpa people
Australia born c.1967
Balangu (sharks) 1989 (detail)
Gochan Jiny-Jirra, Central Arnhem Land,
Northern Territory
natural pigments on eucalyptus bark
64.0 x 139.5 cm

black-headed python (gunungu)
George Milpurrurru
Ganalbingu people
Australia born 1934
Gunungu black-headed pythons 1988 (detail)
Ramingining, Central Arnhem Land,
Northern Territory
natural pigments on eucalyptus bark
232.5 x 80.5 cm

long-necked tortoise (minhala)
George Milpurrurru
Ganalbingu people
Australia born 1934
Long-necked tortoises 1993 (detail)
Ramingining, Central Arnhem Land,
Northern Territory
natural pigments on eucalyptus bark
138.0 x 72.0 cm

saltwater fish (gapila)
Jack Wunuwun
Djinang people
Australia 1930–1990
Artist's father 's Dreaming at Mewirnbi
1985 (detail)
Maningrida, Central Arnhem Land,
Northern Territory
natural pigments on eucalyptus bark
125.0 x 73.0 cm
© The estate of Jack Wunuwun
LPR Maningrida Arts and Culture

The National Gallery of Australia wishes
to acknowledge the Aboriginal communities
and organisations who assisted with the
translations, and Susan Jenkins and
Hilary Hoolihan of the Department of Aboriginal
and Torres Strait Islander Art, National Gallery
of Australia, who compiled the information for
this publication.

Edited, designed and produced
by the Publications Department
of the National Gallery of Australia.

Design: Kirsty Morrison.
Prepress: Pep Colour.
Print: Inprint Pty Ltd.

Cataloguing-in-publication data

And a kangaroo too.
ISBN 0 642 13078 7.
1. Aborigines, Australian-Art-Juvenile literature.
I. National Gallery of Australia.
709.0110899915